THE PR MYSTERY

MAXIMILIAN SAM

MaxSam Communications

Copyright © 2024 by Maximilian Sam

All rights reserved.

No portion of this book may be reproduced in any form without written permission from the publisher or author, except for the use of brief quotations in a book review.

This publication is designed to provide accurate and authoritative information in regard to the subject matter covered. It is sold with the understanding that neither the author nor the publisher is engaged in rendering legal, investment, accounting or other professional services. While the publisher and author have used their best efforts in preparing this book, they make no representations or warranties with respect to the accuracy or completeness of the contents of this book and specifically disclaim any implied warranties of merchantability or fitness for a particular purpose. No warranty may be created or extended by sales representatives or written sales materials. The advice and strategies contained herein may not be suitable for your situation. You should consult with a professional when appropriate. Neither the publisher nor the author shall be liable for any loss of profit or any other commercial damages, including but not limited to special, incidental, consequential, personal, or other damages.

To Jock

My mentor and friend.

Contents

1. An Introduction — 1
2. Demystifying PR — 5
3. Finding Your Hook — 13
4. Perfecting Your Message — 20
5. Strategies And Patience — 25
6. Building A Following — 33
7. Finding Your Media Target — 37
8. The Press Pack — 42
9. The Launch — 50
10. The Snowball Effect — 56
11. Bringing It All Together — 62
12. Planning For Crisis — 68
13. Never Miss A Training Opportunity — 74

14. A Quick Reminder	79
Acknowledgments	82
About Maximilian Sam	87
Books By The Author	90

AN INTRODUCTION

WHY LISTEN TO ME?

I'm incredibly fortunate. My career has allowed me to work all over the world with different cultures and a wide mix of personalities over the past 25 years. I can promise you, no two countries are the same. It's the most common mistake I see. Just because a PR campaign works in the UK, it doesn't mean it will work in Indonesia.

I've now lived in 10 countries around the world, from the UK to South East Asia, with plenty of stops in between. My biggest learning curve came when I decided I wanted to break out of my comfort zone and travel the world. I had to drop all preconceptions and learn about every country I arrived in. It made me far better at my job than I could ever have imagined. The foundations of PR, however, are always the same. It's how we use our skills to target different audiences that changes. I'll give you an example from my other career as an author. The messaging around *It's A Stray Dog's Life* was focussed on the stray dogs in the UK, US and Australian markets. It had to change for the Middle East and Indonesia, where dogs aren't as big a part of people's lives. I adjusted the messaging to being about life lessons for children. Parents have always loved books with a story that helps their children learn the important lessons.

Already, I've given you an insight into this book and the approach I've taken. If you look at the previous paragraphs, you'll see I've told you I've had a 25 year career in PR around the world, including living in 10 countries. I could have told you it all in one sentence. I didn't because it wouldn't have passed the "Yeah and so what?" test. Facts need context. PR isn't a quick fix. It's a long road to telling your story.

Once we've created the backdrop, we can add the facts in. I started by proving I'd had a long career around the world. Now I can tell you who with. I've worked with some of the biggest companies in the world, such as *Saudi Aramco*, as well as some very interesting start-ups, such as *EPMaxx*, and many others in between these extremes. I've covered almost every sector of business you can think of. I even won a bet with an old boss who didn't think I could place a story in *The Undertaker* magazine. I cheated a little as he didn't know my cousin was an actual undertaker! I've worked with some of the biggest multi-national agencies, as well as setting up a couple of my own. I've been in the trenches and on top of the castle.

It's the journey I hope to take you on in this book. I'll try to give you the tools to build your brand and plan ways of communicating it to the world. I'll be describing the essentials of robust and long-lasting communications, as well as giving you real-life examples to highlight each point and stir the creative juices in you.

This isn't a book aimed at giving you boxes to tick. If everyone did the same thing, life would be boring and no communication plan would ever work. We use the foundations in the following pages to give you the platform to be creative in your own way. After all, nobody wants to write a story about the same old thing.

You may, rightly, be asking why I've written this book. It's simple. Since my first children's book was published, I'm frequently hearing authors complain they don't understand PR and find marketing their book difficult. Already, many have made their first mistake. The book is only a product. Themselves as an author is the brand. It's the brand that sells, not the individual product. If people like one of your books, they'll buy others you write because they like the brand you've created as a writer. I realised many business owners, across a variety of industries, felt the same way. People saw PR as a mysterious industry they didn't really understand. I want to lift the mystery to help everyone, including the PR industry itself. The closer the industry can work with clients, the better the results. It involves helping clients understand what we do and why. There are also many things you can do for yourself without an expert on board. I know most authors and small businesses don't have the budget to spend on PR, so any help and advice will, hopefully, help them grow and build.

DEMYSTIFYING PR

LIFTING THE SECRET VEIL

PR, spin, storytelling, or many much worse names. Call it what you will. It all boils down to the same thing. It's about defining your brand and communicating it to the maximum effect. We all do it every single day. The shirt you wore this morning is the perfect example. Why did you pick that shirt? Was it the colour? Is it because it's the only ironed shirt in your wardrobe? There are many questions that will have led to the answer. The only one that matters is the image you are portraying to the world with your choice. Who do you want the world to see you as? The answer is frequently in your wardrobe. It's the very basis of communication. To transfer it to a company setting, it's why the branding colours and logo were chosen. It's the start of a whole process that communicates what people and organisations offer the world. If you haven't worked out who you are, how can you communicate your message to the world? Most of us, as individuals, spend our teenage years (and sometimes several further decades) searching for the answer. Companies do too. It's why there is a healthy business sector in rebranding as an organisation matures and finds its role in an ever changing world.

Understanding how even the smallest detail can affect your brand is the first step on our journey. The second involves a fallacy we need to clear up before we go further. There's a view PR is all about press releases and talking to journalists. We spend time communicating with journalists and use press releases as one of the many tools at our disposal, but it's a very small part of what we do. In fact, much of our job you'll never see. We identify, strategise, and then communicate the DNA of a brand to help build awareness and, by extension, sales. We have a huge toolbox at our disposal to help us communicate, ranging from newspapers, to social media, to podcasts, to just talking to people. They are only tools, though. Without a clearly defined brand and messaging, they won't work. It's like buying a car and not putting fuel in it.

PR is much more than people realise. It's the one area that truly understands a person or business. As we mentioned, it has to. It can't work otherwise. The world will find you out quickly if you're trying to hide behind a false image. Politicians suffer that fate on a daily basis. The speed of social media will highlight it in a flash. It's fine to change opinions and direction. We all do as we gain experience, which can change our views on something. When it happens, explain your change of view. If you don't, the post you shared 15 years ago will come back and bite you. It's where we bump into the most important word in this entire book. Brand. Everything is about the brand. A product is just a subsection of the brand, whether it be a book or an airplane, your customers buy because they know and trust your brand. You wouldn't buy a fizzy drink from Roy's Back Shed Ltd., but you expect to see Coca Cola on the shelf. They may be the same drink, but one brand has built trust over many years, the other is a figment of the imagination (I hope, otherwise my apologies to Roy and his Back Shed). Building and protecting your brand is the most important part of your business. I'm sure accountants would disagree, but they wouldn't have figures to play with if there were no sales if nobody trusted the brand.

I wasn't going to go down the rabbit hole of attempting to define PR. Then I did an internet search and saw the hundreds of different answers to what PR is. It's no wonder people are so confused by the PR industry. For specialists in communication, we really aren't very good at practicing what we preach. I soon realised the problem. People were trying to sound too clever. The adage of KISS (Keep It Simple, Stupid) had been ignored. There's a reason a certain high-selling red top daily newspaper in the UK is so successful. Short sentences with uncomplicated words get the story across far easier than trying to sound clever with long words and complexity. Nobody likes a smart arse. It's why I can give you a simple and clear definition of PR.

PR is identifying the DNA of a brand, creating its messages, and communicating these to the target audiences in the most efficient way.

It really is that simple. If you find someone trying to confuse you with science, it's probably not the science bit that's the issue. Whatever walk of life you're in, being clear with what you're offering is far better than a 50 slide power point presentation. When a brand is leveraged properly, it increases sales, employee retention, and goodwill. It also helps guide other marketing disciplines by giving you the message that defines the DNA of an organisation. It's why your PR, advertising, HR, and other departments should always be in the same room. Each having a different message is confusing. When it's all aligned, amazing things happen. The most successful individuals and companies understand this. It's why they succeed. Everyone knows what to expect from a company when they understand what it is and its direction of travel.

The trick, and the reason people like me have careers, is knowing how to identify and communicate the brand. I see a lot of charlatans offering a PR service online for £125. It gives one press release and limited distribution. It's a waste of money, particularly for self-published authors and small businesses. One press release, even if you get lucky, won't make you successful. They're playing on your fears. A PR campaign is never about instant success. It's about a continuing effort over a long period to build your brand and engage with your audience. Life doesn't give success to cutting corners. Effort and work give you the long-term sales and growth we all strive for.

We're going to go on a journey to show you how to create all the building blocks you'll need, chapter by chapter, showing the importance of each step and giving examples from real-life PR campaigns to give you ideas of how to find your personal or company brand and how to communicate it to the world. It doesn't matter whether you are writing your first book or are the CEO of a multi-national company; the concepts are the same. Budgets may be different, but everyone still wants the best value for money they can get. If you understand the importance of your brand and PR, you'll get far better returns from the investment you put into all your marketing.

There's a lot of work to be done before we even consider spreading our message. It takes a lot of preparation. If you're only thinking about a PR campaign a few days before you launch your book or product, then you've missed the boat. The process starts many months before. One of the first questions you should ask yourself when you have the idea of a new product, book, or publicity campaign is how you are going to market it.

It helps with improving what you're offering, as you can make sure it's something your target markets wants.

The best example I can give involves paper. Not the most interesting product on the planet in theory. It is when someone comes up with an idea that changes the way people look at the product they're buying and see the value you are adding.

I worked with a client from Basingstoke called Wiggins Teape. It's now part of the Arjo Wiggins Group and has long since departed a commuter town in Hampshire. A brilliant brand manager realised people didn't really understand which grades of paper were suited to which job. Which paper is best for your printer? Which for a glossy brochure? It wasn't even a question most people asked. The brand manager came up with a solution. It was called *Paper By Numbers*. It placed every type of paper into a category numbered from one to five, depending on its optimum use. It was simple and brilliant. Automatically, it was obvious it would add value to the customer. Implementing and communicating the concept would be key. The reality was it needed to be fun to capture the imagination. The solution still ranks highly in work I've done over the years. The concept opened the door to creativity, and we jumped straight through.

Our first job was to create a brand hero. Wiggy-T became a character from the planet Paper visiting Earth to explain how we can use one of the most versatile products at our disposal in the most efficient way. The design agency did an amazing job of creating a pool ball with legs and arms to be the guide through the concept. It also meant we could create everything from images to stress balls to get the message across.

The press pack was crucial to our communications plan. I'll explain later the elements you need to include, but it's something that allows you to go deeper into your offering and explain what you're doing to benefit your target market.

We needed something more than flashy images and giveaways. We needed something that would stand out and make people notice, whilst making the concept simple to understand. I'm now going to show my age. We came up with the idea of a cassette tape with a full explanation and a few catchy tunes. Nowadays, we'd do a video on social media, but it wasn't an option back in my younger days when I had hair and a slimmer waistline. I wrote the script in one night. I emailed it to my boss (Yes, email had been invented) at 2am adding I might be late to the office that morning. As it happens, I turned up early as I had another client launch that day. My boss and the team at Wiggins Teape made minimal changes to the script. I'd understood the concept and knew how to communicate it.

It also gave me a day out in Norfolk, where we spent time with the voiceover artists in the recording studio and added the tunes to bring the concept to life. The studio was also doing a promotional campaign for a food company. I walked away with a few freebies that meant the family survived on Mexican food for a couple of weeks afterwards.

The campaign worked on a number of levels. It positioned Wiggins Teape as the authority on all things paper related. It increased sales. It also garnered a huge amount of media interest. We'd succeeded by being creative and planning well in advance to maximise the impact it would make. PR isn't complicated. It takes thought, planning, creativity, and the willingness to go the extra step to make a brand stand out from the crowd. It is labour intensive, but when it works, it generates far more than the cost and effort involved. We can all do generic, but it won't make you stand out. PR is about finding your message and being creative in how you communicate it. It really isn't as scary or complex as many seem to find it.

FINDING YOUR HOOK

WHAT MAKES YOU DIFFERENT?

How dull would life be if we were all the same? Exactly. Everyone is different, whether through experience or education, none of us is identical. It's the same with companies. Every business offers something different that adds its own value. You can argue people make money from copying t-shirts from certain brands, but it proves the point. They are copying brands that already sell. They aren't stealing the product. They're stealing the value of the brand. It's why businesses are protective of their brand. They should be. It takes time and a lot of work to create a brand. Seeing others benefit from your hard work and investment is frustrating at the very least. A brand makes a company stand out, build trust, and sell more products. We wouldn't want our book copied by someone else with them taking the money, so we shouldn't harm brands for exactly the same reason.

What is it that makes these brands stand out and makes people want to copy them? They've created a world around their brand a customer wants to be part of. It aligns with people's values and the image they want to portray in their personal brand. If we take the example of mobile phones, it becomes easier to understand. Would you rather have an iPhone or a Samsung Galaxy? Why? What is it that made you decide? The answer is you wanted one brand more than the other. The functionality could be identical, but you'd still choose the brand you preferred. It's exactly the same argument that's lasted over a century of Pepsi or Coca Cola? They may be slightly different products, but the brands built up around them have been the focus since long before we were born. It's a quirk that when they claim to be better than each other, they both see a rise in market share. One of those things that shouldn't work, but does.

Finding your hook to make you stand out if the most important aspect of anything you can do. It is finding the very DNA of why you are portraying the image you've chosen. An unknown brand launching a product rarely gains traction. A well-known brand launching a product can make front-page news. We've all heard of Virgin. It started as a music shop and has continually expanded since. There have been a few hiccups. Who can forget the wedding service, Virgin Brides? It was one of those ideas that looked good on paper, but was always going to be ridiculed because of the name. A concept died before it had even started as the brand was trying to be clever rather than focussing on the DNA of what it was offering. It shows, none of us gets it right every time.

How can you discover your brand DNA?

There are some crucial questions you have to answer. You can't move on with any of your marketing plans until you do. In fact, you won't have a sales pitch to customers either. People will always gravitate towards a person or product they think will add value to their lives. We all do it. What is even scarier is we always decide based on our first impression. I'm going to make us all feel a little silly now. The two biggest purchases any of us make in our lives are our home and our car. We may read reviews, look at local areas and facilities, or even wander the streets or car showrooms. Mostly, though, we don't. We make these life changing decisions based on marketing, a brief test drive of a car, or a 20 minute wander around a property. We give more thought to which brand of cola we're going to buy. We even, sometimes, take it to extremes and buy a 30-year-old 24.5 tonne ex-Army truck purely by seeing a photo on a website (you know who you are!). It's crazy when you think about it. We're making the biggest decisions based on first impressions. It's why finding your hook is so important. We have one chance to grab people's attention. We need to make the most of it.

To do so, we need to ask these questions: Who are you? What do you do? How are you adding value to your target audience? What proof do you have?

These questions are at the very heart of perfecting consistent messaging for your brand. It helps build trust. There's a reason big and established brands are dominant. We trust them. People buy from those they trust. It's human nature.

The questions I asked are all intertwined. The order I've asked them in is also important. We aren't trying to create a sentence that defines you yet. That comes later. We're giving ourselves clarity on why people should be our customers. We have to dig under the surface to answer these questions. It's always amazed me how many large companies have gone back to the start and realised they needed to change their messaging, as they aren't who they thought they were. It should be done regularly as the world evolves. Is a book you wrote, or product you launched, a decade ago still adding the same value to people's lives in the same way? I didn't think so. There's nothing wrong with changing your message or offering. To do so effectively, we need to find our ever evolving hook.

I'll use myself as an example. Later in the book, I'll show you how I built my author presence and the *Stray Army* brand.

Who am I?

I'm someone who has travelled the world learning my trade. I'm primarily a communicator, but also part sales person. We all are. I'm also far more than just my career. I'm an award-winning author. I used to be a rugby union referee. I'm also proud of the fact I'm almost tone deaf, but have been an international DJ. There's more! I love being out on the water as being a RYA Coastal Skipper proves. I've had a lifelong love affair with both Saracens Rugby Club and Watford Football Club. I'm just about the right side of crazy to not need the men in white coats. My stray animals are also the centre of my world.

It's a lot of information. We will never use all of it. We don't need to. What we are showing is we're much more than just our CV. Everyone is a lot more interesting than they think. We're also all different. It doesn't matter whether we're an individual or a company. Looking in the mirror and answering this first question is the first step in building a robust brand and increasing sales. If you're honest with your answers, then you've identified your hook somewhere. The rest is just bringing it together.

What Do You Do?

The reason we have this book is people have misconceptions about PR. I have spent a lifetime defining who clients are and how they communicate it to the world. We all try to be something we're not from time-to-time. Showing who we really are and what we offer can be scary. It's also the quickest way to build trust with your customers. Putting ourselves in the spotlight is terrifying. It's where most fail, as we're all much happier in the shadows. To be a success, you need to let people see who you are. It's never as scary as you think. Convincing you of that is what I do.

How Are You Adding Value?

The answer is experience. It is more than just having travelled the world doing my job. I add value by helping companies in every aspect of their business. We all have a dream of working for a particular company because of how we perceive them. A major part of my role is bringing all aspects of an organisation together to ensure a consistent message. An advertisement for a job and how people are treated throughout the recruitment process is more important than any press release. People lose trust in a brand because they have a bad experience when applying for a job. You can't hire everyone, but acknowledging an application, being respectful throughout, and not taking months to make a decision will help enhance your brand. A person may not get the job, but a positive experience will see them continue to support you. You also never know when you might need them in the future! This added value stretches to every corner of a business, from the website to social media posts. Everything can influence the story you're telling the world. I warned you PR was more than just headlines in a newspaper.

What Proof Do You Have For Your Claims?

Surprisingly, we've already mentioned many of the proof points. I've lived all over the world. I've worked with some of the biggest companies out there. I'm also an award-winning author which shows I know how to tell a story.

We now have all the pieces of the jigsaw. We just need to put them together correctly to form the picture we are trying to portray.

Perfecting Your Message

Identifying Your Elevator Speech

You may well have seen a tool called a messaging house. If not, it's worth looking online, as they can be very useful in a multitude of ways. They are adaptable in helping you write the blurb on the back cover of your book to proving there's a market for your product.

In essence, the messaging house gives you a roof, walls, and foundations. We'll go through them from top to bottom, but you can actually fill the boxes in any order that suits your thought process. The reason I start with the roof is it highlights quickly whether the messaging you have is right or wrong. Obviously, if you're doing this in textbook fashion, always build a house foundation first! If you fit the pieces together correctly, the outcome will be the same. We'll look at each level and then give an example.

The Roof

This will be your one or two sentence elevator speech. It refines your hook to a short statement which defines who you are, what you do, and how it adds value. I mentioned I often start here to see if the walls and foundations can support the roof you've built. It's an eye-opening experience, as you find what you thought described your brand doesn't actually stand up to interrogation. The process, though, will give you ideas that had been elusive.

The Walls

Without these, there's nothing to put the roof on. This is where we define who you are, what you do, and how it adds value. We split the wall into three sections. One for each question. We answered the questions in the previous chapter, so it shouldn't be too difficult to fill this part in. When you have it is important to underline the strong keywords. These are the words or short phrases that will build the roof. It's where the definition of the brand comes from.

The Foundations

Everything is built on foundations. Without them, a house will fall down. In this instance, they are your proof points. You need to prove the statements you are making on the walls. If you can't, then your statements are wrong, which makes your elevator speech incorrect.

I know people will shout at me for saying you can fill in a messaging house in any order you want, as a house should be built from foundations up. They have a point, but starting the process from different angles gives you a perspective you might not have thought of. Playing around will give you a far better insight.

However, rather than driving the final nail into the coffin of my career, I'll follow perceived logic in the example I give. I am going to be intentionally vague with the answers as it will, hopefully, make it easier to understand.

First, my proof points for who I am.

1. I have 25 years' experience in PR, putting me firmly in the veteran category.

2. I have worked all over the world.

3. I have won awards for my children's books.

These proof points allow me to make a statement on the walls.

1. I'm a PR veteran with over two decades of experience around the world.

2. I'm an award-winning author of children's and adult fiction.

You'll see how this fits into the roof at the end.

Second, the proof points for what I do.

1. I've worked with organisations of all sizes around the world.

2. I've defined the core messages for many companies.

3. I've devised and implemented communications plans.

This leads us to our statements.

1. I identify and communicate key messages of brands and products.

2. My career has given me global knowledge on how to maximise the impact of communications plans.

Third is how I add value. Again, we start with the proof points.

1. I spend time understanding every aspect of a business.

2. I introduce systems to ensure consistent messaging.

3. I increase brand recognition, increasing sales.

This gives us our statements.

1. I increase brand recognition and sales.

2. I devise systems to ensure messaging is consistent across the company.

We now need to add the roof. For this, we only need to look at the keywords we've put in place. As such, we come up with one or two sentences where we can prove every claim we're making.

"I am a PR veteran with over 25 years' experience around the world, as well as being an award-winning author. I identify and communicate an organisation's core DNA, leading to increased brand recognition and sales."

If you've followed the building blocks this far, then we've reached our first goal. We've defined who we are and what we offer. All we need to do now is work out how to communicate it to our key audiences.

STRATEGIES AND PATIENCE

PLAN, PREPARE, AND BE PATIENT

I can't emphasise enough how PR requires patience. You will not become world famous overnight. If you did, you'd have huge problems with supply chains, new product development, and your sanity. If you look at all the successful brands, they've built sustainably over time. How often have we all searched for the most popular toy at Christmas only to find it sold out everywhere? Instant success is an issue that can destroy your brand if your target audience can't get hold of your product. It may sound counter-intuitive, but you need to control your growth so you can keep all your customers happy and coming back for more. Even the great J. K. Rowling wasn't an instant success. It takes time.

Authors are the worst for this. Many write one book, do well, and then don't have any follow-up for customers to spend more money. We all need a range of products for customers to buy and to keep them returning to our brand. It's a lot cheaper and less labour intensive to retain customers than it is to continually go out and reinvent the wheel. Patience, while frustrating, will lead to the sales and recognition over a far longer period than being a flash in the pan. The longer you're around, the more brand trust, sales, and money in your back pocket will be created. Unless, of course, you want to be a one-hit wonder. In which case, I wish you luck and hope you're called Harper Lee.

It's why patience is a human's biggest skill. We have to build it into our strategy to maximise our communication with the world.

We've already worked out who we are and what we offer. Now we need a plan to tell everyone.

No strategy is ever identical. How can it be? If we're all doing the same thing, there's nothing to talk about. Our strategy is our opportunity to be creative and stand out from the crowd. There's an old saying, "Fail to plan and you're planning to fail." PR is the proof point confirming some wise words.

How do we create a strategy?

The first lesson is to start as early as possible. Waiting for publication or product launch day is crazy. Customers need time to buy into whatever you're selling and understand your brand. You'll need to create a "buzz" before, during, and after your launch.

This is where PR learns from the advertising industry. Have you ever wondered why you see the same television advertisements repeatedly? It's psychology. The average person only remembers an advertisement after they've seen it seven times. Repetition is crucial to breaking into the human psyche. Your PR strategy needs to reflect this. The key to this is defining your audience. You need to get your message in front of them as frequently as possible.

We always start with a soft approach to introducing a brand. We need to build trust so customers are open to buying your new product from a brand they've already built a relationship with. Think about your first thought when someone mentions baked beans. There are plenty of suppliers, but I bet Heinz was top of your list. Trust is how we sell products. Get yourself out there with interviews and news so people recognise you. You need to position yourself as an expert who customers will gain value from. It comes back to your messaging. Why should people listen to you? Quite simply because you're an expert in your field.

Creating a list of target media to feature in whilst we wait for the product is how you'll gain advance sales and a successful launch day. Trailing cover, or packaging, designs is a quick fix to keeping people interested. Use what you have and generate the "buzz".

We are also lucky to live in an age where we can create tools with no expense other than our time. What is it that makes people trust a brand? If you've already answered that, the next part will be obvious.

Trust is built on your customers believing they know who you are and what you stand for. You don't need a new book or product launch to build trust. What you need is something your customers can be part of. Step one, before you've even finished plotting the final iteration of your product, is to get a website up and running. There is no excuse not to. Some major players in the market offer name, hosting and decent design software for free. If you want to purchase your own domain name, personalised emails, and hosting, it's still incredibly cheap. Ecommerce and payment packages can increase costs, but they're a direct investment in your company if you are aiming to sell directly to your customer through your website. I'm no web designer, but even I had the website for *MaxSam Communications* up and running in under a day. If you have the budget, then there's nothing wrong with using a specialist to help you. I know, from experience, we all need to manage the best places to spend the money we have. PR, a website, advertising, and fulfilment processes are all vital to a business. You will need to decide the ratio you use them in to maximise return on investment.

Why is a website so vital?

This is where a strategy appears. A website gives us a platform to talk about our brand. It also gives us much more. This is where we can host our blog. The importance of this regular column cannot be underestimated. It's your chance to build the bond with your customers and also give them the special status of being the first to hear your news. Customers will feel an attachment with you and click the subscribe button. It's a vital way of giving you a direct link to contacting them. It means you can send them emails with the latest news, special offers, or, even better, a regular newsletter.

The more customers feel connected to you, the more they'll buy. There are plenty of reputable suppliers to manage your customer lists without you having to worry about the legal maze of data protection.

We now have your key jobs months before any launch. Sort out your website, write a blog, and build your customer lists. Remember to use all your social media to highlight the latest blog posts, the website, and news. Building excitement and a following means the foundations are in place to see success long before you have anything to sell.

Stage two is the most exciting, and stressful, part of a strategy. How are you going to launch your product? There's no definitive answer. It depends on what you're selling. A new financial investment package will have a very different launch than that of a new skyscraper. I know because I stood on the roof of Tower 42 taking photos of the topping-off ceremony of The Gherkin in London. I'm not great with heights, so the memory has stuck with me. As has the television coverage we gained.

We'll talk in details about the launch later. One thing to remember is, if it can go wrong, it will. Don't worry if things aren't perfect. Ask any theatre actor if they are word perfect for every performance. Of course they aren't. It's one day on a long journey. You'll laugh about the mishaps years later. If you're smart, you'll even have turned them to your advantage.

Stage three is the rest of our lives. A book, especially, never dies. We need to create a strategy to keep people engaged with the brand. Success can come in days or in years. As long as it arrives, the timing is of minimal significance. As long as sales are paying the bills, your breakthrough will come. It could be you were just ahead of your time and the world needed to catch up. Alternatively, the behavioural change of customers could be a long process. Our challenge is to keep customers engaged, however short or long the process might be.

The most important part is to continually engage and show how your brand is adding value. Blogs, interviews, events, and giveaways all play a part. As do many other tools at our disposal. It takes a lot of work to keep the "buzz" around your product. If you don't, people will forget and you won't need an accountant to tell you you've made no sales.

This book isn't meant to give you a boring checklist to follow or to show you every tool at your disposal. It's impossible to do so. However, the strategy is so important, I'll give you an outline checklist to follow.

One year in advance:

Perfect your messaging.

Build your website.

Start your blog and newsletter.

Start building your subscriber lists.

Position the brand as an expert with interviews, comments on social media, and flash stories about the brand.

Join social media groups in your target area.

Three months before launch:

Plan your launch, even if it's only online.

Devise giveaways, if you have the budget. A friend has recently published a book. She wrote a shorter introduction book that she uses as a free giveaway. It encourages people to buy her book as they now know the background to it.

Write your press pack.

Engage with people who might review your product. Third-party endorsement is gold dust.

Try to remember launch day is the moment your idea comes to life. Enjoy it.

Post-launch:

Keep the "buzz" going with blogs and newsletters.

Identify awards to enter.

Never turn down an opportunity for an interview that speaks to your target market. If it doesn't, you can turn it down.

Keep checking and promoting the key messaging we came up with. Consistency and repetition works.

Building A Following

Raising Excitement in Advance

We can now turn to the part of the book that becomes more practical than theoretical.

We have our message and a strategy. If we don't communicate it, who will know?

This chapter will highlight why it's so important to start the process early. A following doesn't appear overnight. It takes communication, hard work, and interaction with your audience. It is true, it's rarely been easier. Social media gives everyone a platform. Certain changes are now making it more complex, but in the main, it's a vital tool for everyone.

Social media might give a platform to everyone, but that's also its weakness. You have to stand out. Otherwise, you're just another face in the crowd. There are many tricks you can use, but at the heart of all of them is consistent communication. That's the easy bit. The algorithms built into social media sites promote posts and articles that add value to their users. To be brutal, neither I nor anyone else cares what you had for breakfast. People want information that can help them in their lives.

I'd rather not create a pathway to everyone doing the same thing, but there's a very simple way of increasing your following. Think of your favourite quotes and describe how they relate to your business or product. You can create a library of them which will use quotes people are familiar with to highlight how your brand stands out and create the consistent messaging we're looking for.

More importantly, with social media, make sure you interact with others. If someone has posted something about your specialist area, comment on it. You are trying to show you're an expert in your field, after all.

The final lesson with using social media is to be selective. There are too many platforms for anyone to focus on all of them fully. Think which ones are going to give you the most engagement with your target audience and pick two. Put most of your energy into these and continually check you are speaking to potential customers. It all becomes a little pointless if you only ever talk to competitors, as they're unlikely to buy your product.

This doesn't mean you should ignore other platforms. Far from it. It's better to ensure your focus is on the areas you'll get the most return for the investment of your time and money.

How do I know this works? I've recently helped launch a company purely using LinkedIn. The company offers a specialist service. It was clear from the outset the founders were already linked to many in their target market. Placing quotes and deeper articles helped build a following almost entirely made up of potential customers. The trick was making sure every communication added value and conversations we posted on were relevant and highlighted the expertise of the company. Not every PR campaign needs national newspaper coverage.

To add value to our social media, and traditional media for that matter, we need more. A regular blog keeps you in your customer's thoughts and gives the opportunity to build a deeper relationship with them. Newsletters used to do this before the digital age kicked in. They are still a valid way of communicating, albeit they are more likely to be delivered by email these days.

The secret to a good blog is one that gives information to people, but also makes them want to interact. If people are engaged, you've done the hard part of making them a customer. If you get it right, strange things can happen. One of my author blog posts was even reprinted in a newspaper. It happened purely because it was interesting and added value to people.

To keep the consistency of messaging, plan your next six months of topics in advance. A last-minute dash will invariably lead to something either boring or totally disassociated from your brand.

Finally, make sure your blog gives a deeper insight into who you are. People buy from other people. How often do you hear "it was the personal touch"? The more people think they know about you and trust you, the more engagement leading to more sales.

All this talk about social media doesn't mean you should forget traditional media. Newspapers, especially local ones, magazines, podcasts, radio interviews, and television are still our lifeblood. I've even ended up writing unrelated articles for publications, but always under my name. It allows you to share them in your blog and on social media. It all adds credibility and can show more of who you are and your interests. Try to avoid politics or religion, though. They provide a minefield where even the stoutest of heart fear to tread.

The lesson from this chapter is simple. Choose your platforms and keep your message consistent. The following will build far faster than you expect.

FINDING YOUR MEDIA TARGET

WHO DO YOU WANT TO SPEAK TO?

Knowing which newspapers, magazines, and news outlets to target is the part of PR most people seem to have issues with. It's hardly surprising, as it's the most labour intensive part of the process.

Reputable PR agencies have a secret weapon. When I started my career, the secret weapon comprised four lever-arch files filled with every publication and journalist in the UK, and many from around the world. Every month, new pages would arrive when journalists moved jobs. We used to scour them using keywords to build our media lists. Nowadays, it's much easier as companies offer online versions. Sadly, if you aren't a PR agency, or have access to a friend, the budget for access to these lists is prohibitive.

It's an incredibly labour intensive job, so you can understand why it may seem expensive. There are free, or low-cost, ones online. In my experience, they are of limited help. They tend to be incomplete and outdated. It's why you should also beware of people offering cheap press release services. The press releases won't be targeted and the distribution list will have little bearing on reality. People's time costs money. If you use a PR service, expect to pay for it. Those in the industry have to eat as well.

How can we find the contacts we need without it swallowing our entire budget in one go? There's no shortcut, is the answer. It's going to take a lot of time and use of your favourite search engine.

You probably know some of the more famous titles in your target area. You are an expert in your field. You will have read some of the relevant trade publications. If you're a property developer or investor, for example, you'll have read *Property Week*. If you pick up a physical copy, you'll find a list of contacts inside. Journalists don't just go looking for stories, they need us to go to them too to fill the pages. It's why they make their preferred contact details available.

Sadly, we're looking for more than one contact. It's why it takes time. A slight shortcut involves using your search engine. Type in the keywords describing your target audience and add magazine or newspaper. It will give you a list of the most popular titles and potentially even give you links to podcasts, radio, and TV shows. It won't be definitive, as there will be smaller titles it might not pick up. It's not the perfect solution, but it's one of the most effective ways we can build a list.

We then need to visit every website. It will ensure the publication is what you're expecting. There will always be a contact link to send news. Invariably it will be newsdesk@publication.com. These are closely monitored email addresses. They also become hugely overcrowded. You're going to need to stand out.

There are many ways to grab a journalist's attention. Many of them are contactable on social media through their work accounts, or at the very least, by phone. I've placed thousands of stories over the years purely by contacting a journalist and asking them if they'd be interested in a story about whatever the topic is. My favourite example involved something I still do every morning with a cup of coffee. I read the newspapers and relevant websites to see if there's anything I can "piggyback" for my clients. One morning I found a story in a national newspaper saying most people would work in a call centre in their lives. It was perfect for one of my clients as they supplied software to call centres. I called Sky News and three hours later my client was in the studio at Isleworth giving a live interview. The newspaper had given me a hook. I knew how to maximise it. I did have an advantage. I'd previously spent several weekends working as a runner at Sky News, so knew exactly who to call. It pays to know how both PR and the media work.

If you communicate with a journalist and you've got your messaging right, then most of the time they'll say yes to your story and give you a contact email to send the press release to. You've already primed them for the story. It's almost guaranteed media coverage. I promise it works. You've helped a journalist do their job by not wasting their time and providing useful content. Everyone wins.

There are two golden rules you must never break. Journalists have more deadlines than most of us have hot dinners. Work out when these deadlines are likely to be and avoid contacting them in the hours prior to it. Disturbing them in the race to a deadline will not make you friends.

The second rule will see contract killers sent after you if you break it. Never ever call a journalist and say, "Did you get my press release?" it doesn't sell your news and, almost certainly, gets you added to the dreaded "avoid at all costs" list. Do not do it. It doesn't add value and creates huge annoyance.

We've also run into our first problem. There is no way we can contact every single publication on our list. You don't need to. Most of what you've put together is a wish list. You need to identify the top 10-15 publications and target them with communication in advance. The rest can be sent the press release on its own.

In a similar way to social media, identifying key publications is vital. They should be the ones your potential customers are most likely to read. They are going to be on your target list for years to come. Treat them well and nurture a relationship with them. Every journalist has a "rent a quote" list. Be the person they always want to talk to.

For those further down the list, make sure your covering email is compelling. If you stand out, a journalist will write about your news. Nobody wants to read something boring, so don't expect a journalist to write about something that hasn't caught their imagination.

The same system works across all media. It does, however, ignore our secret weapon. Friends and contacts. Ask them if they know anyone in the areas you're targeting. You'd be amazed at how many have the contact details you need. Networking is an underrated skill. Use it. It pays off.

The lesson to learn here is there's a lot of labour intensive work to find what you need. Social media groups, friends, and contacts are your secret weapon. Use what you have at your disposal. People, in general, enjoy helping each other.

THE PRESS PACK

WHAT A JOURNALIST NEEDS FROM YOU

We now come to the nitty-gritty part. Planning ahead will make it easier. It will also save weeks of your life further down the line. The press pack is an investment in your future success.

A press pack can be split into two areas, which makes it easier to understand. The final part changes with every piece of news you have. We'll get into the guide of how to write a press release shortly.

You are going to need some good quality images. A picture tells 1,000 words. I've obtained media coverage purely by having good quality photos or graphics to give to the picture editor. It's a route many never think about. If you have eye-catching imagery, you've created an extra opportunity to get your story used.

An example is some work I did for a client in the UK. They'd installed the largest indoor poster seen in the country at the time. It was the size of two double decker busses. the description and imagery made it very easy for publications to run the story. It's an important tool, so make sure your images stand out. It won't be the only place you can use them.

The second part of the press pack requires less upkeep. You will need to update it from time-to-time, but large parts of it will remain the same. This is where we can keep an in-depth background, FAQs, headshots, and anything else you are going to use to market your product. It's also the perfect place to keep a secret weapon. It can be incredibly time-consuming answering written interview questions from journalists. Think about the regular questions you might be asked and answer them. You now have a base document to answer media enquiries. It also provides an excellent briefing document when preparing for face-to-face interviews. Preparation is key to everything, making this a useful trick to know.

We now have the key components of the press pack, although keeping potential giveaways close at hand also helps.

The most common question I'm asked is how to write a press release. For some reason, many people have a mental block over it. It's actually like riding a bike. Once you've got the hang of it, it's easy.

The two key areas you are trying to address with a press release are that it is interesting to a journalist, and it contains the information they need to build a story. Don't worry about not having everything you want to say in a press release. If you've made it interesting, with enough information, a journalist will contact you if they need more.

A press release should always answer the key questions. Who? What? Where? When? How? and Why? If you've answered those, you'll have got your message across in an interesting way without even trying. To show you how it works, I'm going to use the press release my alter ego, Maximilian Sam, distributed to announce the publication of *It's A Stray Dog's Life*.

The most important line you will write is the headline. It needs to immediately grab a journalist as interesting. Otherwise, it's in the bin before they read any more. Always remember, journalists are incredibly busy with more deadlines in a week than most of us have in a lifetime.

The version of the press release we'll use is the one targeted at the English-speaking Turkish media.

British Ex-Pat, Maximilian Sam, Publishes First Children's Book.

The headline has given the immediate hook of being local and relevant, whilst announcing news. A journalist will read further as it fits the type of story they write about. It means you are already 90% towards getting your story printed.

The first sentence should reinforce the headline whilst adding key information.

Local British Ex-Pat, Maximilian Sam, will publish his first children's book, It's A Stray Dog's Life, about the stray dogs he looks after on 28 February.

We have already added more substance to the story by telling a journalist we have a children's book coming out on 28 February, the title, concept, and the audience. It's taken two short sentences to create and describe a story the target journalist is likely to be interested in. It's also been easy to do as we've used our key questions to define what information we need to include.

You will notice the headline, and the first sentence would not work for the media in Hertfordshire, for example. It's difficult to be a British ex-pat in Watford. It's why it is important to identify your target journalists and make the headline and first sentence appeal to their key audience. Amazingly, we've just discussed the only part of a press release that needs changing to suit your different targets. For example, we changed the headline for the Hertfordshire media to:

University of Hertfordshire Alumnus, Maximilian Sam, Publishes First Children's Book.

Obviously, the start of your first sentence will change to reflect this too. As we mentioned, we now have press releases targeted at different markets without having to reinvent the wheel.

The rest of the press release is straightforward. The next paragraph you've already written. It's the elevator speech describing your news. For an author, it's even easier as it's the back cover blurb. The elevator speech is the DNA of your story. You've already written it, so what waste it?

Have you ever wondered what dogs are thinking when you look at them? Now you can find out, as Princess, Buster, and Snowy share their adventures. It's A Stray Dog's Life follows the stray dogs as we get the chance to see life through their eyes.

We've described the product we are selling. It means we're now onto the last part of the main body of the press release. This is the opportunity to add personalisation and snippets you haven't included already. It's also the part most people I've taught struggle with the most. It's time for a quote.

Maximilian Sam said, "I look after several stray dogs in our area, giving them food and taking them on walks. I've been able to watch how they interact with each other and humans. It's what gave me the idea for the book. I also wanted to create something that wasn't a picture book, but also not as grown up as Harry Potter, for example. As such, each chapter is 1,000 words long with seven chapters per dog. This makes it perfect for a week's bedtime reading about each individual dog."

We've now explained why we can write about the stray dogs from a position of expertise, and why we wrote the book in a certain way. We've given a journalist plenty of information and an opening if they'd like more. Everything is there to write a piece announcing the publication of *It's A Stray Dog's Life*.

There is one more important area to add. It should always be titled *Note To Editors*. This is where you can give your own background and contact details, as it's the part journalists don't print. If you don't put *Note To Editors*, you might find your email address and phone number printed too. I've seen it happen.

Maximilian Sam is the award-winning author of three books. He has spent his life travelling the world, living in 10 countries so far. He now splits his time between working, writing, and looking after his stray animals. You can find out more about Max at maximiliansam.com. If you require further information, images of the front cover of the book, or a photo of Maximilian Sam, please email xxxx or call xxxx. You can also click the WeTransfer link to download images.

We've now given a little background on who you are and pointed the journalist towards further information. You can also add in further information. If you've won an award, mention it.

We have mentioned images for your press pack. You should have several which you can also use over your social media sites. If you try to send them as an attachment with a press release, the email server will almost certainly block them, preventing your news from hitting a journalist's desk. Embedding images doesn't work either. Pointing out in your email images can be downloaded from a reputable file sharing website is far more effective. I'm happy to give a gratuitous plug to WeTransfer here. I've found them to be the best of the best.

Our press release and images have now hit our target audience. What more do we need in a press pack?

You and your company are the star of the show. We need a document to give a deeper dive, explaining who we are, where we come from, and why we offer what we do.

In another quirk of fate, you've already written the opening and outline in the *Note To Editors* part of your press release. In technical terms, use the boilerplate you've created. Waste is pointless. Reinventing the wheel is time-consuming and frustrating. You can use leftover roast chicken to make a lovely curry. Why not use what you've already created?

You can expand on it and go into more detail. Your CV, or the way you described your idea in a business plan, is an easy way to give deeper insight. One rule is to keep it to a single page. We have other documents that can expand further. We don't want a journalist to feel they don't need to do an interview as they already have enough information. This is where our secret weapon of the briefing document comes in. It has a plethora of uses. It's our FAQ document, our media interview preparation, and our cut-and-paste base for written answers. You will need to update it from time to time, but it's worth its weight in gold.

You now know how to write your press release and compile your press pack. It's going to save you a lot of time further down the road.

The Launch

An event or soft launch?

We have lift-off. It's launch day. This is the most stressful day of the process. The adage of "if it can go wrong, it will" is bang on the money.

Don't be scared. Launch day is just a blink of an eye on a very long journey. Consistency and sustainable sales are key. We'd all rather still be making solid sales in ten years than be a flash-in-the-pan, making a quick buck that we fritter away at the after party. If you match my feat of being taken to accident and emergency to have five stitches in a finger wound whilst worrying you'd spilt blood on a Brazil football shirt signed by Pele, then I doff my cap and welcome you to the club.

The key to a launch event is identifying your budget and sticking to it. It can cost you anything from zero to millions of dollars. It all depends on what you are launching and who you are trying to speak to. Let's look at two examples at either end of the scale.

I have many author friends. It's not the most effective way of making money, so budgets are always tight. Spending nothing other than your time is the best way to go for many. Unless you're a very famous author, the chances are you will not get journalists to a launch anyway. It's more likely to be an expensive celebration party. There are smarter ways to fulfil your goals. This is where technology is our friend. There are many groups who host guest days for authors online. It involves answering people's questions on social media throughout the day. A far easier task than it sounds because we already have our Q and A document from our press pack. It entices your potential audience and allows you to make a deeper connection with them. Bookshops and customers are frequently happy to help where they can. They like feeling connected to a brand they see as successful.

When we launched *Paper by Numbers*, we carried it out in a customer's shop. It comes back to people enjoying being connected to success. It also helps build a stronger customer base. It drives relationships between customers and suppliers. Find and use the champions of your brand, as they are already your biggest supporters.

There are also numerous networking groups who offer a platform for small businesses. It comes down to research to find the ones that work best for you and your product. I have used these to end up as a regular guest on podcasts and other platforms. It's the same as social media, your research finding the niche areas that talk to your customers is never wasted. You can see, by networking, how you can launch a product or service for free. It takes hard work and dedication, but so does your business. Always remember, you probably don't need as many customers as you think to be successful. Giving your customers what they want and making them feel part of the journey will lead to a sustainable business and ever-increasing sales.

There's always the other end of the scale. One highlight of my career was working on the launch of Marina Bay Sands in Singapore. It is a stunning complex and already a mainstay of the Singapore skyline. Its highlight is an infinity pool on the roof. If you get a chance to visit, even a trip to the viewing platform is worth it. I'm not sure I felt the same when I had to run from one end of the complex to the other in 40 degree heat and high humidity to accompany a journalist doing a piece to camera. For someone who had quit major exercise a few years before, I didn't end up looking my best. Thankfully, I was behind the camera and not in front.

The launch involved inviting 1,000 journalists from around the world. The press conference was a logistical masterclass in itself. It also highlighted how there are some things you can't control. A journalist posted a story on his newspaper's website. It was a great piece of writing, accompanied by a photo of the high-level infinity pool. The same couldn't be said of the comment of the first reader.

"The pool is really dangerous. Someone could swim off the side!" Unsurprisingly, it is impossible to do so. There will always be someone you can't convince.

The three-day event included free climbers racing up the outside of the building, tasting sessions with Michelin starred chefs, and various other events to highlight everything the resort has to offer, including the first licenced casino in Singapore. I'm still amazed the whole thing passed off with no major incidents.

It's not always the case. There are times the best plans fail. I had a CEO fly from the US to the UK for several media interviews. He was going to be talking about logistics. We'd planned everything, including having his favourite soft drink available. We couldn't have planned for the major train crash happening that very morning. I was grateful to the transport editor of the Financial Times for taking the time to call me and make his very reasonable excuses. Thankfully, the US CEO understood, and we rearranged things. It shows things sometimes go wrong. All you can do is stay calm and think of an alternative solution. These things happen. Don't blame yourself for things out of your control.

I've seen some amazing launches in my time. A recent one involved a supermarket chain. They generated excitement about their new store opening with posters and a leaflet drop in the local area. Even they were surprised by the crowds which built up outside the new store on launch day. It was a hot day, so juice, water, and cake were handed out in the queue. Common sense prevailed, and they opened the doors early to ease the pressure on the crowds. If they'd had someone collapse in the heat, the story would have been very different. The decision making ensured it was a hugely successful launch.

Conversely, I've recently watched a hotel launch from the outside after huge amounts were spent on the refurbishment. A disaster understates how badly things have gone. The hotel still has external areas that haven't been painted. As a 5 star ultra inclusive, the lack of attention to detail is astonishing. Things started to go awry during the soft launch. The hotel wishes it had a private beach. It doesn't. The bullying tactics used by security led to the police attending as locals staged a sit-in on the beach. The police sided with the locals. It's never a good look when locals, guests, and beach users see several police at your hotel. I won't go into further detail, but the hotel has never been busy since it opened. A lack of a plan and marketing is costing the owners a lot of money.

This is the greatest lesson from all these examples. For a successful launch, you need a plan and to stick to it.

Things will go wrong. They always do, but clear decision making and ideas for a fallback strategy can turn even the worst scenario to your advantage. Ensure the launch will speak to your target audiences and then budget accordingly. An online launch with minimal spend can be just as effective as a huge budget. Finally, launch day is one day on a long journey. Don't worry if it isn't perfect. There'll be time enough to rectify anything that didn't go to plan later.

THE SNOWBALL EFFECT

CARRYING ON THE MOMENTUM

How do you know when your PR campaign is working? It's almost impossible to measure precisely as it isn't a concrete product. Other factors, such as advertising, also deserve some of the credit. How can you measure the impact of these things? There are some very smart tools available that give a good idea, but, in truth, whatever anyone tells you, you can't measure PR precisely. Hits on your website or social media pages can provide clues, newspaper and magazine coverage shows whether you're heading in the right direction, but you also have to be careful as these can be misleading too. It's why only the desperate pay money for extra followers on their social media pages. It's pointless. Why would you? It won't make you more sales or increase influence. It certainly won't get you closer to your target audience. There is an infatuation with follower numbers on social media, but it is the worst way of judging if you are being successful. Are all those followers your target market, for example?

The only real way of knowing if your influence is increasing is if sales and recognition of your brand are increasing. If they are, then your marketing and communication is working. If you are being invited to appear on podcasts or give comments for articles, then you have hit the sweet spot. It's called the snowball effect and started long before you saw the results.

You've hit the point where all the hard work is paying off. You are getting opportunities to tell your story because people see you as an expert in your field. Your brand is in demand. The snowball effect has kicked in.

Seeing a brand we have built snowball is the big buzz we are all searching for. It gives a huge business advantage as we are now the first port of call when an expert is needed for a comment in your specialist area.

In the days before social media, PR was easier. Step one was the press release. This led to the story becoming bigger, with us being able to comment in feature articles. The final step was always a bylined article discussing our specialist area and our brand. In effect, every news story we had gave us a three-month lifespan.

The world has changed.

A story announcing the launch of a book or product now lives forever. You can update older blog posts to create discussion and interest. Admittedly, I'm still amazed one of mine was used word perfect in a newspaper. It shows the power of having something interesting to say and positioning yourself as an expert in your field. It also means we have far more control over our brand and who we speak to. Conversely, the extra noise in the marketplace means we have to work harder and smarter to be heard.

Remember, you set up your business because you are an expert in your field and have a compelling story to tell. It is why newspapers, magazines, radio, television, and podcasts, amongst others, should talk to you.

Third-party endorsement and consistent messaging convinces your target audience to become part of your brand universe. Once they are in, they will buy everything you are selling because they trust you and know what to expect from the brand they've become part of.

It's the same reason this book started with an introduction outlining my credentials. It proves I'm an expert in my field. It gives you a reason to buy my books. The introduction was the starting point for building the snowball effect as we've gone through chapter by chapter.

It may be a good time to revisit your messaging. Are you certain what you are saying about your brand is correct? Can you prove it? The messaging around your brand is the golden key to success. If it's wrong, you have a far bigger mountain to climb to be the successful business you hope to be. If it is right, it is the closest to guaranteed success you will ever find.

One very good example springs to mind from the literary world. Memoirs are the ultimate PR messaging tool for authors. They are talking about a lived experience, after all. If you would like to find a few, then I can highly recommend the We Love Memoirs page on Facebook. It's incredibly friendly and gives a range of amazing choices of memoirs to read. The example I'm referring to comes from someone who has become a very good friend. Jaqueline Lambert is certainly one of those whose life contains plenty of stories. She, along with her husband and four dogs, changed their lives by selling everything and buying a camper van to spend their lives touring Europe. Her series of books, *Adventure Caravanning With Dogs*, are superb.

The snowball effect kicked in when they bought an old Army truck and converted it into a very large camper van. The Beast was born. Her book, *Building The Beast; How (Not) To Build An Overland Camper*, is a cross between Grand Designs and Top Gear. It's all about the trials and tribulations of the conversion. It created a snowball effect because her author brand already positioned her as an expert on living and travelling in a camper van with husband and dogs for company. She's now appeared in numerous publications and on TV. She's also won awards for her books. She's even being mentioned by other authors in their books. The brand expertise has been seen and the exposure grown from there. It's the perfect case study.

The snowball effect is incredibly powerful. It gives consistent third-party endorsement as an expert. Customers follow those they believe in. The equation is very simple.

How do you create the snowball effect? The clues can be found in the previous chapters. It won't happen overnight. It requires a lot of work to build and position your brand. If the building blocks are in place, and you've communicated them, then it will happen as a natural extension of your PR and marketing strategy.

The secret is consistent communication. Customers need to know what they are buying and, as has become more important in recent years, what your brand stands for. Customers need to know you have the same ideals as them, whether that be environmental or the way you treat your staff. It's become as important as the product you are selling. It's why it is as vital to get job advertisements right as it is a press release. Every piece of communication matters. It's the same with news shared internally or newsletters. Never say something you'd be worried about if someone found it left behind in the back of a taxi and read it. Your messaging must be consistent whatever the platform.

It is the main reason creating the snowball effect is so important to your business. A press release will tell part of your story, but, as the snowball rolls down the hill and gets bigger, the more opportunities you get to tell your deeper story and build trust in your brand.

The fallacy of PR being just a press release should be shattered by now. There is so much more. Everything we've built throughout this book is focussed on giving a snowball the chance to gather momentum as it rolls down the hill to generate brand growth and increased sales.

PR isn't as much of a mystery as it seems. It just encompasses far more than people realise.

BRINGING IT ALL TOGETHER

MAXIMILIAN SAM AND THE STRAY ARMY

When the pandemic struck I, like so many other, found myself in limbo. People saying it would last two years terrified me. What was I going to do if I couldn't fly off to a new job and another adventure?

The answer was to follow my dream. I've wanted to write a book since I was a little kid. Now I had the time to do it. The book was the easy part. I only had to watch the stray dogs on the beach to come up with plenty of stories. There was one common theme as I set about building the brand before publication. Everywhere I turned, I saw authors claiming they were becoming stuck with the marketing side of things. It's not a surprise as the literary market is the most crowded space in the world. Selling one copy should be cheered from the rooftops when you sit and think about how much competition there is. I did some research to see if it was just authors having these issues. It wasn't. Marketing is the part of any small business that can see it succeed or fail. The problem is a lack of funds for small companies and start-ups coupled with the plethora of other jobs that need doing to keep a business running. It proved to be the major driver to write this book to show people how they can help themselves and find a level of budget to obtain help when they needed it.

This is also where the brand specialist kicks in. I knew, before I even started writing the book, I'd be doing more than one, so devised a brand to build everything around. My two nephews held the key to the name. Maximilian Sam was born. A slightly unusual name with the benefit of the web address being available.

I wasn't stopping there. My original books were aimed at children and told the stories of the army of stray dogs I look after. Welcome to the *Stray Army*. I knew books alone would not make me rich. I needed something more. Merchandise always has the potential to make money. T-shirts, baseball caps, and much more besides are now available bearing the *Stray Army* and *Maximilian Sam* logos. My first piece of luck came in the form of WeTransfer, a file sharing platform I've used for years. Beta testers were required to create a sales platform using WeTransfer. It meant I'd be able to provide downloads and charge for them. There are now short stories, signed photos, and posters available to download from the website. As there is minimal overhead, the cost is cheap as people can print every item at home, or have them as their screensaver. I've taken a single book and created an ecosystem surrounding the brands.

I also needed a platform for my day job in PR. *MaxSam Communications* was born. It enabled me to bring together all my global experience to offer services to small businesses. We've even created special author centric packages at hugely reduced rates as a thank you to a community that's supported me throughout my journey as an author.

I'd created the brands, but how was I going to bring it all together? It's fine having the names, websites, and a brochure, but if nobody sees them, then it's pointless. The answer comes down to the old mantra of hard work. It's very true you get what you put in. It's great having all the bells and whistles, but pointless if you do nothing with them. It's like owning a valuable painting but never looking at it.

In this book, I've given you many of the tools required, ranging from the press release to the press pack and much more besides. I, thanks to my many years' experience, went a lot further. I identified not only our target market but also publications, podcasts, and influencers who could get the message across to potential customers. I've done countless interviews, made easier by the Q and A document in the press pack, appeared as a guest on several podcasts and videos, as well as finding book reviewers who have, to a person, been amazing. A review about *It's A Stray Dog's Life* containing the sentences, "this is so goddamn heartwarming. Mommy's go and buy it," is always going to help. It means the brands are backed by third-party endorsement from journalists, to reviewers, to podcast hosts.

The momentum still takes time to build. I got very lucky in two instances.

A Turkish neighbour is a senior university lecturer. She wrote a paper on *It's A Stray Dog's Life*. Apparently, it's very good, but even the English translation had too many long words for me to really understand it. It is an amazing thing, though. How many UK authors can say they've had a paper written about their book from a Turkish university? Add it to the posters still hanging in several restaurants and a couple of pet shops and you can see how I sold a few copies in Turkiye too.

The second stroke of luck was having a lifelong friend who is a teacher in the USA. An hour on a video call with a classroom full of 9-year-olds was terrifying. They were incredibly smart. It gave me a whole new audience, so much so the book is now being translated into Spanish. With such a large potential market in the USA and Spain, it holds a lot of promise.

These steps have also led to a few surprises along the way. I am now a regular on *Daisy Lane Publishing/KidLit International's* Inspire video series talking about all things books. Obviously, my speciality is the marketing. It contains authors from around the world, so the exposure is incredibly powerful. My efforts have also led to fulfilling a childhood dream. I grew up wanting to be a journalist, before I moved to the dark side. I followed my own advice and contacted my local newspaper to ask if the first book would be an interesting story for them. Of course it was. I sent over the press release and saw my book on the front page a week later. Two and a half years later and I now write a weekly column for my local newspaper. The brand building highlighting my experience paid off, as they knew I could write and understood how newspapers worked. PR can make dreams come true.

I still have other plans in the pipeline, including networking events, car boot sales, and craft fairs. It all takes work, but sometimes having a presence and talking to people is still the best way to make sales. I know it's certainly worked for me when I've chatted to holidaymakers on the beach. It's amazing how many have bought the books, purely because they met the author.

You can now see how the processes I've given you in this book do work. If we put the effort in, follow these processes, and gain the odd smattering of luck, it pays dividends. The effort is worth it as you see sales increase and your business grow. It just takes a touch of patience.

Planning For Crisis

It's Only a Crisis If You Haven't Prepared

In life, things go wrong. Best laid plans can implode unexpectedly. Ask any sports team. A loss out of the blue happens to us all. Thinking of these setbacks as a crisis is short-sighted. Every bump on the road is also an opportunity. It all depends how you react to a setback. The key is always the three Ps.

Preparation, preparation, and preparation.

Of course, none of us can prepare for every eventuality. Life doesn't work like that. We can, however, cover the obvious issues we might face. Devising plans of how to deal with issues that arise and having answers at the ready can turn a concerning moment into an opportunity to show your company can rectify things when they go wrong. It's amazing how positively customers react to a quick and honest response. However bad it may seem, honesty and clarity can turn a crisis to your advantage.

There are actually very few things in this world that constitute a crisis. The main cause is humans either not being prepared or going into a state of panic that exacerbates the problem. The more common problem is better referred to as an issue. As with any issue in life, a calm head searching for solutions, rather than ranting, almost always turns what looks like a problem into something that positions you in a better light to those around you. A solution always makes a problem disappear.

I had an issue that could easily have ballooned into a crisis and driven a wedge between myself and one of my best friends. I made sure he understood his mistake, but then turned it to both our advantages. He took photographs of pages of one of my books and posted it to social media. There was no reference to the book, title, or author. It was, in effect, being passed off as his work. I was less than amused, and that's before we thought about the copyright issues. Thankfully, taking a deep breath and ensuring he took the offending post down sparked an idea. I took the short story he'd photographed and created a free download from my website. The cover carried the logo of his restaurant and links to all my books. We even gained local media coverage for it. We'd turned a silly issue into something positive for both of us, just by keeping calm and thinking about of a solution rather than focussing on the problem.

There are some things that are a crisis the moment they happen. My career in PR started with one. A man walking into a school with guns and killing young children and a teacher will always rank as a crisis. For many, I was on the wrong side of the debate as I worked for the gun lobby. Thankfully, I wasn't in the USA, so, after an initial difficult period driven by shock and grief, we spoke to many of the parents who lost their children. Some are still friends to this day. I can never imagine what they went through. The empathy and understanding prevented everything from becoming worse for all sides of the discussion. It was amazing how much everyone agreed upon. Those who enjoyed the sport of shooting and the related industries were tired of being cast as pariahs. They'd been calling for changes to the law for years. The parents wanted assurance an event like this could never happen again. The fact they were willing to have intelligent conversations to find common solutions speaks volumes about them as people. It took something so shocking and emotive for the UK to now have some of the most stringent gun laws in the world. It's now incredibly rare for there to be mass shootings on British shores. The correct result for all and a high-profile crisis that ended up solving problems other countries still struggle with. Discussion, empathy, and an honest reaction prevented a knee jerk reaction that wouldn't have solved the problems for anyone.

For the record, I have never been good around guns. They really aren't my thing. Even though I'm apparently a pretty good shot, it's something I never contemplated getting involved in. It's an important lesson when hiring PR consultants. You want them to focus on your business. If they disagree with what you sell, then they shouldn't have been meeting with you in the first place. If they are working with you, their prejudices get left outside the door.

The most important lesson when confronted with a crisis or issue is to only give out confirmed information. A crisis is a living, breathing thing where things change by the minute. If you say something unconfirmed, it will hurt you. Emotion needs to be removed and rumour be kept away from the information vacuum. When you can give out confirmed information, it gives the basis for making informed decisions and turning any problems into opportunities.

You might think a crisis or issues can't or won't happen to you. I hate to burst your bubble, but if you don't prepare, it will happen. It can be anything from a misspelled word in a book to a bad review or production issues with what you're trying to sell. There are many things that can go wrong depending on your business.

An example of why burying your head in the sand is a bad idea comes from a client I once had in the industrial sector. He even complained to my boss that I was constantly pushing to complete the crisis pack.

They had paid for it, after all. He was convinced there was nothing that could go wrong. Three days after his complaint, things went wrong. My client disappeared, as he did not know what to do. Thankfully, the CEO and the rest of the comms team were very good. Dealing with the crisis was messier than I'd have liked, but we came through relatively unscathed. It highlights why preparation is vital.

Preparing for a crisis is relatively simple. Obviously, the bigger the organisation, the more complex it becomes as you end up with a phone book of contacts who need to be activated or kept informed throughout. If it's a big enough organisation, you might have to have the backup of a hotel conference room on standby in case something prevents the use of the office. Technology has helped alleviate this problem, but always be prepared. For most of us, we will never need to take those factors into account. What we need to do is sit down and work out the most common issues that could affect our business and work out how we respond to them. What will we say to customers? What will we say to suppliers? What will we say to the media? And most importantly, what will we say to our employees?

Once this is done, all you need is a document clearly defining each person's responsibilities. Who will speak to who? Who is working on solving the issue or crisis?

Dealing with a crisis isn't difficult. People and emotions make it go wrong. A calm head, even if it means you have to go into the bathroom and scream for a moment, will provide solutions and opportunities.

NEVER MISS A TRAINING OPPORTUNITY

PR, MEDIA, AND PRESENTATION TRAINING ARE KEYS TO SUCCESS

We've all had bosses who think they know everything. Even an hour of management training wouldn't have gone amiss. It's a fault in the corporate world that people are rightly promoted for being good at their jobs, but are not given the tools to be successful in a more senior role. I even had a very senior PR person tell me he wasn't very good at the soft skills. A terrifying concept when you realise PR is more about people than just about any other industry. It's crazy when you think about it all.

It's why training is so important. There's a certain amount we can learn from experience, but the reality is we all need a helping hand from experts and some training from time to time.

PR offers training that's useful to small businesses, authors, global CEOs, and especially politicians.

The most common thing we're asked to help with is media training. People are scared of the media, when they have no reason to be. We've already shown preparation is key. If you know, and believe in, your messaging, the rest is simple. The golden rules are to stick to your messaging and KISS. I don't mean sexually assault a journalist. That would lead to a crisis. Keep It Simple, Stupid. You need journalists and your target market to understand and buy into your brand and messaging quickly and easily. Blinding people with science invariably makes them fall asleep and makes you look silly. There are opportunities to look clever. Whilst trying to get your message across in an interview isn't one of them.

Every business needs people who have been media trained. It's not just for talking to the media. It helps when talking to potential customers, too. The old line of "I was media trained years ago" doesn't work. You need to practise and a refresher course never goes amiss. It reminds me of the funniest training session I ever ran. One member used the aforementioned line and the day being a waste of his time. If he'd been media trained properly, he'd have known he was wrong. His arrogance was getting on everyone's nerves. He was going to learn the hard way. A part of media training involves role play where I act as a journalist. We record the video and critique it afterwards. If he was so good, he shouldn't have a problem with an antagonistic interview. It turned out he wasn't that good. It took just three tough questions before he stood up and threatened to hit me. Order was quickly restored. He'd learned a vital lesson. He was a really nice guy and paid the penance of the bar bill after training without complaint. It proves the point. Never become so arrogant that you think you know it all. None of us does.

There have been many other laughs over the years. Calling someone at 7am before their training session pretending to be a journalist only to be told, "give me a minute, I'm in the shower" was a highlight. I've heard of taking two bottles into the shower, but a mobile phone?

There's a lot of my life that revolves around clients making presentations and speeches. It's far harder than a media interview as the audience in front of you is bigger. It's easy to understand why people are scared of it. I suppose my days as the chair of my university's Drama Society eased many of my nerves. The truth is, we're all nervous. The key is knowing how to control the nerves.

The first rule is one that governs everything. Know your message and communicate it. For most, a script won't work. One mispronounced word on a script can knock even the best off their stride. You are better off with three key points on a piece of paper and working your way between them. It's also key not to over prepare. You'll come across as stilted and boring if you do. You're aiming for natural and knowledgeable. A talking text book is never a good look. We also need to slow the heart-rate and adrenalin. The most common mistake is people speak too fast. A pause when presenting can feel like a lifetime. To the audience, it's a split second. You can borrow my trick in a 60 second speech I made to be elected communications officer at university. I didn't say anything for 45 seconds. It felt life several lifetimes. The only sentence I uttered was, "Silence happens when there's no communication." It saw me elected. It was the hardest speech I've ever made. The silence was really difficult. It highlights, in an extreme sense, why pauses and slowing your pace are your friends. You'll come across in a far better light and people will listen rather than getting lost in the trap of rapid machine gun fire delivery.

There are two key tricks to helping with public speaking. The first, breathing in and counting to ten before exhaling slows the heart-rate and adrenalin flow. It calms your nerves. There's nothing wrong with having to do it a few times before you go on stage. The second is to always have a friendly face in the audience. A smile to show you're doing OK goes a long way. Confidence is crucial, so use a friendly face to build yours.

There's also PR training. This book is almost an introduction to the course. If you understand the concepts behind PR, then you can maximise not only your own efforts, but those of consultants and agencies you use. If anyone ever pitches PR services to you without either offering a few hours in your office, a video call with the whole team, a true and understandable breakdown of what input they need from you and how the team will work, or an introduction to PR and how to maximise your investment, then I'd be looking elsewhere.

PR is the industry that looks into the very soul of your business. You can use training courses to identify strengths and weaknesses and help your business grow. You'll also grow as a person and learn skills you'd never have considered. It highlights why you should never miss a training session.

A Quick Reminder

What have we learned?

First, it's clearly impossible for me to write a book with 13 chapters. It's the only superstition I have. Every chapter has relevance, whether you're doing your own PR or learning how to work effectively with a consultant or agency.

The most important lesson is to know the basics of how PR works and the foundations it's built on. We all expect PR people to understand their client's business. It works both ways, as the more you understand, the more you will get the results you are looking for, and the greater your return on investment. If there's something you don't understand or are unsure of, just ask. The smartest people I know aren't the ones who have the most knowledge. They are the ones who know how to ask when they are unsure of something.

Remember, PR is not an instant solution. It's a tool that builds your brand over time. You'll have successes along the way, but all of it adds up to your brand growth over time. I still get a buzz from seeing media coverage or one of my bylined articles in the local newspaper. I'm also aware each piece is only a small part of the jigsaw that makes up my brand.

Patience is a virtue. Very few of us are born with it as a skill. It's something we learn through experience. Would you rather be the Rolling Stones still touring decades later, or a one-hit wonder?

We now know how to write an effective press release, research contacts, sensibly use social media and create our messaging. It takes time, but it's one of the most important investments you can make.

None of these tools will make you rich and famous on their own. It's a mix focussed on your target market. The mix can also include advertising, direct email, and many other marketing tools. If you get it right, the snowball effect happens. You'll be a guest on podcasts, radio, and other places sooner than you think, as your brand message will have positioned you as an expert with knowledge to share that's useful to others.

It's why the most important lesson is to focus on your brand. A product will sell because of the strength of your brand. It's why you frequently hear businesses talk about the market share of their brand. If the brand and messaging are strong, you can sell anything to anyone.

Take a breath. Grab a pen and paper and learn some lessons from this book. Interrogate your brand and adjust areas where required. It's how you will pay the bills and grow a successful, sustainable business, whether that be as an author or in any other field.

Success isn't a gift. It takes hard work, patience, and a certain level of skill.

I wish you the very best of luck. If you need some help, or just a chat to talk things through, feel free to drop me a line. Unlike most, I don't charge for everything. Sometimes life is about building relationships rather than cash.

Acknowledgments

The bit where I say thank you

I have to start by saying a huge thank you to the man who set me on my journey in PR and allowed me to have this often crazy life travelling around the world. Bert Burns was an amazing man with a talent for bringing the best out of people. Who would have thought my birthday dinner with my parents, Bert and his daughter Melanie, my then girlfriend, would end up defining my life? He arranged for me to spend a week with his PR company to see if it was a career I wanted to pursue. One week turned into two years. I was thrown in the deep end working for our client, The British Shooting Sports Council, in the aftermath of the horrific school shooting in Dunblane. It gave me an amazing grounding in PR. However many thank yous I say, it will never be enough to show the respect I have always had for Bert. I still remember Melanie calling me after my first day to see how it had gone. The care and support shown is a cornerstone of how a law graduate with no idea of what he wanted to do with his life has thrived and seen the world.

There are many others who've had a lasting effect on my life. This book is dedicated to an amazing friend who guided me and taught me so much. We made a fantastic team, especially when the laptop broke down and we had to make up a new client pitch as we went along. Thank you Jock.

Berkeley Communications in Reading will always bring back many happy memories. Chris Hewitt, David Tutin (and his wife Victoria) made it a time filled with laughter, friendship, and the discovery of a pub with no name.

A huge thanks must also go to Hill & Knowlton, especially Andrew Bone, Brian Shrowder, Marwan Abu-Ghanem, and Steve 'Wilbur' Wilson, who gave me my first role abroad in Saudi Arabia. The respect I still have for everyone there at the time is huge.

Two other people stand out in my career. Brian Devlin took me under his wing and mentored me. His calming influence brought out the best in me for which I'm eternally grateful. James Baldwin has become a great friend. I'm not sure if it's because of the great work we did together or because he's still the only person to send me an SMS asking to meet at The Loving Hut. Turns out it was a very good vegan restaurant!

My author journey has introduced me to some incredibly talented people who have become good friends. Jacqueline Lambert, Sue Bavey, Alyson Sheldrake, and Jane @Tweetables feel like the sisters I never had. I can't thank you enough for the support and laughter you've brought to my life. It would be remiss to not thank Gary Cockaday, whose debut novel *Full Circle* is amazing. He's a lovely guy and a huge supporter of everything I do.

I'm not sure I'd have survived this life if it wasn't for some amazing friends. Phil Waley, Jeremy Church, Rupert Englander, and Rico form an amazing team around me. Add in the constant friendship of Suresh Pulandaran and it becomes obvious I'm a very lucky man.

Also to my Turkish expat friends, John and Karen Simpson, Della and Tony Droy, Burcu and Aurora, and my best mate Resit.

Journalists play a major role in my life. Hasan Bayrak, Andy Probert, Jan, and everyone at Voices Newspaper in Didim relit my love of PR and the media. Allowing me to write articles for the paper was the match that relit the fire. On a similar note, thank you to Lucille Shone at The Ege Eye. Both newspapers have been my biggest champions. Thank you from the bottom of my heart.

To Peter, Justin, and Carlos at the Do Not Scratch Your Eyes Podcast, thank you for allowing me to write about Watford Football Club. Your personal support behind the scenes, alongside club legend Luther Blissett, saved me during some very dark days. I'll get to the Bunker one day. When I do, the beers are on me.

Daisy Lane Publishing has given me the chance to appear on video podcasts to talk about marketing. It's introduced me to even more incredibly talented people who teach me so much and make me laugh a lot. Huge thanks to Jennifer Sharp for taking the plunge and inviting me on to your Inspire Series. I'm in awe of the talent in your videos and very grateful for the friendship everyone has shown me.

I can't miss out the friendliest group on Facebook. We Love Memoirs is full of amazing people sharing their stories and lives. It's incredibly supportive and friendly. I promise I have a memoir in the pipeline to share with you soon enough.

A huge thanks to the team at WeTransfer. An amazing group who enabled me to add an extra dimension to the Stray Army universe. I am forever in your debt.

I couldn't do any of the things I do without the support of Mum, Dad, Greg, Pavla, Sam, and Max. My family is the centre of my universe. I love you all to the furthest stars and back.

Finally, where would I be without my stray animals? You give me so much more than I can ever repay.

Chris Evans

2024

PS. I've developed a habit of including some advice purely to make sure you're still reading.

Jump in headfirst when an idea to take you out of your comfort zone arises. You could end up travelling the world. I did.

Also, thank you to the amazing friend who said they'd give me a job making the coffee if this book turned out to be career suicide. I always need a back-up plan!

ABOUT MAXIMILIAN SAM

Maximilian Sam is an award-winning author of two children's books and a compilation of short stories. The idea for the children's books came from the number of stray dogs and cats he currently looks after. It's not unusual to find him walking ten dogs on the beach and feeding four or five cats in an evening. The *Stray Army* brand shows what can be achieved from a standing start, whether you're a sole practitioner or multi-national organisation. Max is now able to sell everything from t-shirts to lunchboxes alongside his books.

He has over 25 years' experience in communications around the world. He started his career in his home country of the UK, before gradually moving further east. His first stop was Saudi Arabia, where he ran an office for a multi-national PR agency. He then progressed to Indonesia, before heading back to the Middle East and stops in Qatar and Bahrain.

He currently works with both companies and individuals around the world helping them communicate and grow their brand.

As well as spending a career in communications, he has also worked as a freelance journalist. He's written on topics ranging from Watford Football Club, to animal welfare, to articles about the little village by the sea he currently lives in.

He founded the MaxSam Group to bring together his three main businesses:

1. MaxSam Communications

2. The *Stray Army* brand

3. His author persona of Maximilian Sam

You can find out more about MaxSam Communications at https://www.maxsamcommunications.com/

You can find out more about Maximilian Sam's books and The Stray Army at https://www.maximiliansam.com/

- facebook.com/authormaximiliansam
- goodreads.com/author/show/22204253.Maximilian_Sam
- instagram.com/authormaximiliansam
- linkedin.com/in/maximilian-sam-a689031b8/
- twitter.com/maxsamauthor
- youtube.com/channel/UCMJ4VC4iCo-YSHlnWkY_EPQ

BOOKS BY THE AUTHOR

UNDER THE PSEUDONYM MAXIMILIAN SAM

It's A Stray Dog's Life

Have you ever wondered what dogs are thinking when you look at them? Now you can find out as Princess, Buster, and Snowy share their adventures in this multi-award winning debut.

It's A Stray Dog's Life 2

You can now meet Mumsy as she tries to control her two puppies, Pitch & Putt; join Jasper in his new home in Izmir, and help Toby solve complex crimes.

Stories From A Stray

Come and join a stray on his journey through life in this series of short stories.

You can find out more about Maximilian Sam at

www.maximiliansam.com

www.ingramcontent.com/pod-product-compliance
Lightning Source LLC
Chambersburg PA
CBHW070159230526
45471CB00002B/735